WHY DO WE SAY THAT?

101 Idioms, Phrases, Sayings & Facts! The Origins & History Of Your Favorite Expressions, Phrases & Proverbs

---

SCOTT MATTHEWS

Copyright © 2023 Scott Matthews

All rights reserved. No part of this publication may be reproduced, distributed or transmitted in any form or by any means, including photocopying, recording, or other electronic or mechanical methods, without the prior written permission of the publisher, except in the case of brief quotations embodied in critical reviews and certain other non-commercial uses permitted by copyright law.

Trademarked names appear throughout this book. Rather than use a trademark symbol with every occurrence of a trademarked name, names are used in an editorial fashion, with no intention of infringement of the respective owner's trademark. The information in this book is distributed on an "as is" basis, without warranty. Although every precaution has been taken in the preparation of this work, neither the author nor the publisher shall have any liability to any person or entity with respect to any loss or damage caused or alleged to be caused directly or indirectly by the information contained in this book.

The more that you read, the more things you will know. The more you learn, the more places you'll go. - Dr. Seuss

Contents

Introduction — vii

1. The grass is always greener — 1
2. Busybody — 2
3. On the same page — 3
4. Let the cat out of the bag — 4
5. Add insult to injury — 5
6. Pardon my French — 6
7. Beat the clock — 7
8. In your element — 8
9. Pull strings — 9
10. Blow hot and cold — 10
11. To have sticky fingers — 12
12. Pull a Houdini — 13
13. Toot your own horn — 14
14. On a shoestring — 15
15. Easier said than done — 16
16. Doggy bag — 17
17. A sandwich short of a picnic — 18
18. Right off the bat — 19
19. On thin ice — 20
20. Smell a rat — 21
21. Low man on the totem pole — 23
22. Up in arms — 24
23. Full of beans — 25
24. Play by ear — 26
25. Crème de la crème — 27
26. An eye for an eye — 28
27. Stick one's neck out — 29
28. Touch base — 30
29. New ground — 31
30. Hold the fort — 32
31. At face value — 34
32. Swan song — 35
33. Heart misses a beat — 36

34. Feel like death warmed up	37
35. Fair dinkum	38
36. Fish out of water	39
37. Rings a bell	40
38. Get out of hand	41
39. Go back to the drawing board	42
40. Sleep with the fishes	43
41. Skid row	46
42. Hard pill to swallow	47
43. No brainer	48
44. Chip off the old block	49
45. Stuck in a rut	50
46. Knee jerk reaction	51
47. Shot across the bow	52
48. Ground zero	53
49. Packed like sardines	54
50. Best of both worlds	55
51. Lose your marbles	57
52. Eager beaver	58
53. This ain't my first rodeo	59
54. Fifth wheel	60
55. Cut corners	61
56. Bear a grudge	62
57. Chasing rainbows	63
58. Down for the count	64
59. Hop, skip, and jump	65
60. In hot water	66
61. Rose-colored glasses	68
62. On the ball	69
63. Yada yada	70
64. On cloud nine	71
65. Spin doctor	72
66. Foaming at the mouth	73
67. A left handed compliment	74
68. Fool's errand	75
69. On his last legs	76
70. Shotgun wedding	77
71. In the fast lane	79
72. Fortune favors the bold	80
73. Looking to your laurels	81
74. You can't judge a book by its cover	82

75. Big fish in a small pond	83
76. Pipe down	84
77. Ins and outs	85
78. To move at a snail's pace	86
79. Go cold turkey	87
80. Burn one's boats	88
81. Pony up	90
82. Face the music	91
83. A hairsbreadth	92
84. You look like a million dollars	93
85. Green fingers	94
86. Don't give up your day job	95
87. The jury is out	96
88. Game the system	97
89. Hand Over Fist	98
90. Call it a day	99
91. Oddball	101
92. Six of one, half a dozen of other	102
93. At a crossroads	103
94. Hail Mary	104
95. Hot to trot	106
96. Cold-hearted	107
97. Clear as mud	108
98. The devil is in the details	109
99. Take to the cleaners	110
100. If worse comes to worst	111
101. Graveyard shift	113

Introduction

Are you ready to explore the intriguing world of idioms? You might be surprised to learn that we use them daily, sometimes without even realizing it! But have you ever wondered about the origins of these fascinating phrases?

Also called idiomatic expressions, idioms have slowly been introduced into the English language as it has developed over time. These expressions have a commonly understood meaning which varies from the literal meaning of the words being spoken, read, or written.

As we explore the origins of idioms, we'll be taking a journey back in time to discover what the English-speaking world was like when these phrases were first used. While some idioms have clear origins, others have evolved over time, passed down through oral tradition, and may have unknown origins or multiple theories of where they came from. Despite this, the enduring popularity and widespread use of these idioms continue to pique our interest and inspire further inquiry.

So let's dive right into the wonderful world of idioms and where they come from!

1. The grass is always greener

There are a few theories about the origin of "the grass is always greener." It perhaps originated from the practice of comparing one's own lawn or grass to that of a neighbor's. Another theory is that the phrase originated from the practice of grazing livestock. Sheep, cows, and other animals are naturally inclined to move on to greener pastures as soon as the grass they are eating becomes less lush. This behavior led to the idea that the grass is always greener on the other side of the fence. The expression has morphed into the idea that people often compare their own lives to the lives of others and find them wanting. People tend to think that others have it better than they do, whether it's a better job, a better partner, or a better home. The phrase is now widely used to describe the tendency for people to envy or covet what others have and to overlook or underestimate the value of what they already have.

2. Busybody

The term "busybody" refers to a person who is excessively or unnecessarily involved in the affairs of others. It originated in the 16th century and likely comes from the concept of being "busy," which has long been associated with being productive and active. In the context of the idiom, a "busybody" is someone who is constantly poking their nose into other people's business, often without being invited or welcomed. This can be seen as intrusive or annoying, as the person is not minding their own business but rather constantly trying to be involved in the affairs of others. Oftentimes, saying that so-and-so is acting like a "busybody" is a negative way to describe someone who is overly nosy. However, it can also be used in a more lighthearted or playful manner to refer to someone who is simply very curious or interested in the goings-on of those around them.

3. On the same page

The origin of the phrase "on the same page" is a topic of much discussion, with some speculating that it might have come from choral singing. In choral singing, it is essential for all participants to be in harmony and to sing from the same sheet of music. However, it is much more likely that this idiom can be attributed to business and educational settings, where copies of a single document or material are distributed among a group, and all members are required to be reading from the same page in order to effectively understand and discuss the topic at hand. The expression is employed to describe a situation where people are in agreement and working towards a common goal. This phrase has been in use since the early 20th century and it has become popular in the context of business, politics, and other fields where people work together. It implies that everyone is in agreement and that there is a shared understanding of the situation.

4. Let the cat out of the bag

"Let the cat out of the bag" is an idiom that has been in use for centuries. It originated in the 18th century, when markets were a common place for buying and selling goods, including animals. Unscrupulous merchants would often try to deceive buyers by substituting a cat for a piglet and selling it in a bag. If the deception was discovered, they would "let the cat out of the bag," revealing the surprise and ruining the sale. This practice gave rise to the idiomatic expression, which is now used more generally to refer to any situation where a secret or surprise is revealed prematurely. The first literary reference to the phrase can be found in *The London Magazine* in 1760, indicating that the expression was already in common use at that time.

5. Add insult to injury

To "add insult to injury" describes a situation in which someone makes a bad situation even worse by doing or saying something hurtful or offensive. The phrase suggests that an initial problem or injury is being compounded by an additional, often intentional, affront. This term is extremely old, it comes from one of the fables told by Aesop, who lived in Ancient Greece. The story, "The Bald Man and the Fly," is about a bald man who gets bitten on the head by a fly. He attempts to thwart the fly by striking himself on the head, but ends up hurting himself more. The fly then flies away and makes fun of the bald man, saying that if he's willing to hurt himself like that just to get back at an insect, what will he do to himself for insulting himself, too? The point of the story is that revenge only ends up hurting the person seeking it.

6. Pardon my French

"Pardon my French" is an idiomatic expression that is used as a polite or humorous way of apologizing for using profanity or strong language. The phrase is believed to have originated in the 19th century as a reference to the use of profanity in the French language, which was considered more acceptable than in English-speaking cultures. One of the earliest recorded uses of the term was in a story published by Karl Von Miltie in 1831 in his book *The Twelve Nights*, where he writes: "My dear Mr. Heartwell, you are come to see me at last. Bless me, how fat you are grown!—absolutely round as a ball:—you will soon be as embonpoint (excuse my French) as your poor dear father, the major." In this example, Karl is not apologizing for the insult, but rather for using the French word "embonpoint" to describe someone's weight. This illustrates that the phrase can be used not only to apologize for profanity but also for using a foreign language. It can also be employed in a humorous way, to mock the idea that French is a more sophisticated or refined language.

7. Beat the clock

To "beat the clock" means to finish something within a certain time limit or before a deadline. It is commonly used in the context of a race or competition, where the goal is to complete a task faster than one's opponents. The origin of this idiom is thought to be related to the popular television show *Beat the Clock*, which aired in the United States from 1950 to 1958 and was later revived in the 1970s. The show featured a series of challenges or stunts that contestants had to complete within a certain time limit in order to win prizes. The earliest use of the phrase outside of the show dates back to 1952, in an article published in the *Chicago Daily Tribune*. The article mentions the television show *Beat the Clock* and refers to the expression as a "catchphrase."

8. In your element

When someone tells you that you're "in your element," it means you are comfortable in your surroundings. The expression came from the Victorian era, where all things were classified as belonging to one of the four elements; earth, fire, air, and water. The idiom means someone is in a situation where they can use their skills, abilities, or interests to their full potential. It suggests that the person is comfortable and confident in their surroundings and is able to excel or perform at a high level. The origins of this phrase are somewhat unclear, but it is thought to have come from the ancient Greek philosopher and scientist Aristotle, who believed that everything in the universe had a natural place or "element" where it belonged and functioned best. Today, the expression is used more figuratively to describe someone who is comfortable and confident in a particular situation or environment and is able to excel or perform at a high level. It is often used to express admiration or respect for someone who is particularly skilled or talented.

9. Pull strings

The expression "to pull strings" means to use one's influence or connections to get something done. The phrase originated in the late 1800s and comes from the idea of manipulating the strings of a puppet to make it move. In this context, pulling strings refers to controlling someone or something to achieve a desired outcome. The idiom is commonly used to express influence or connections in a political or business context, as it implies that someone is using their power or resources to get things done in a secretive or underhanded way. The term is also used to describe people who use their connections to gain an advantage in their personal life.

10. Blow hot and cold

The idiom "blow hot and cold" refers to a situation in which someone is inconsistent in their behavior or opinions. It's thought to be derived from the ancient Greek philosopher Aristotle's observation that people with fevers would often alternately feel extremely hot and very cold. In this context, the phrase referred to the idea of fluctuating between two extreme states or conditions. In modern times, the expression is used more broadly to refer to any situation in which someone is indecisive in their behavior or opinions, and can be applied to a wide range of situations, including relationships, career decisions, and other areas of life.

Did You Know?

The longest hiccups on record lasted sixty-eight years.

Humans are the only animals that produce tears when they cry.

The human body contains enough fat to make seven bars of soap.

The Great Barrier Reef, the world's largest coral reef system, is visible from space and is so large that it can be seen with the naked eye.

There is a type of jellyfish called the immortal jellyfish (Turritopsis dohrnii) that is capable of reversing its life cycle and becoming a juvenile again after it reaches sexual maturity. This means that it has the potential to live forever, as long as it is not eaten by a predator or subjected to other forms of mortality.

11. To have sticky fingers

The idiom "to have sticky fingers" means to have a tendency to steal or take things that do not belong to you. It is often used to describe someone who is dishonest or prone to stealing. There are three different theories about the origins and history of the idiom. The first theory refers to the way in which thieves might use their fingers to take small items without being noticed, leaving behind a sticky residue on the stolen item. The second theory is that it may be a reference to the way in which people with a sweet tooth might get a sticky residue on their fingers when eating candy or other sweets. The third suggests it may have originated in the gold mining industry, where workers used sap or honey on their fingers to collect gold dust and then pocketed the value of the gold when it was weighed for payment. Nowadays, the phrase can be used in a serious manner when referring to criminals, or in a mild manner like referring to a child who frequently takes others' toys.

12. Pull a Houdini

The phrase "pull a Houdini" refers to someone who is able to escape from a difficult situation or confinement. The expression is derived from the name of the famous magician and escape artist, Harry Houdini, who was known for his death-defying stunts and ability to escape from seemingly impossible situations. Houdini began his career as a magician in the late 19th century, and quickly became famous for his spectacular illusions and escapes. He would often perform stunts where he would escape from handcuffs, straitjackets, and even from sealed containers such as milk cans and packing crates. He was also known for his ability to escape from prison cells and other confinement. The phrase "pull a Houdini" first appeared in print in the early 20th century. A fun fact about the magician and escape artist Harry Houdini is that he was a skilled aviator. Houdini purchased one of the first airplanes in America and taught himself how to fly it. He even performed aerial stunts and tricks as part of his magic act.

13. Toot your own horn

The expression "toot your own horn" means to boast or speak proudly about one's accomplishments, skills, or achievements. We use it when someone is openly praising themselves or drawing attention to their positive qualities. The phrase likely originated from the act of musicians blowing their own horns to get noticed during a performance, which symbolizes self-promotion. While its exact first use in writing is unclear, the idiom's concept has been present in various cultures for centuries. Over time, its meaning has evolved to encompass not only musical talents but any form of self-promotion or bragging. Today, we use "toot your own horn" both playfully and critically, reminding each other to be humble and let our accomplishments speak for themselves, rather than boasting excessively.

14. On a shoestring

The idiom "on a shoestring" is used to describe a situation where resources are limited and tight budgets are involved. The exact origins of the phrase are not entirely clear, however, it has been in use since at least the 1800s. One theory suggests that the phrase originated from the idea of a shoestring being thin and not very strong, and therefore, not able to support much weight. The metaphor is that if one is living on a shoestring, they are living with very limited resources and are not able to afford much. Another theory suggests that the idiom may have originated from gambling game "faro," where a "shoestring gambler" referred to a petty, tinhorn gambler who only had limited resources to gamble with. In modern context, if a household is on a "shoestring budget" then the family is struggling to make ends meet and might need to take actions like cutting expenses, working extra, shopping thrifty, and other methods in order to save money.

15. Easier said than done

The phrase "easier said than done" means that a task or action may sound simple or straightforward when discussed or suggested, but it is actually much more challenging or complicated to accomplish in reality. We use this expression to convey that verbalizing a plan or solution is far less demanding than the actual implementation. The origins of this idiom can be traced back to ancient proverbs and sayings that highlight the gap between words and actions. While its exact first use in writing remains unclear, similar phrases have appeared in various cultures throughout history. Its meaning has remained consistent over time, emphasizing the difficulty of translating ideas into practical actions. Nowadays, we use it to acknowledge the complexities and obstacles involved in turning intentions into achievements, serving as a gentle reminder to approach tasks with a sense of realism and determination.

16. Doggy bag

A "doggy bag" or "doggie bag" refers to the container of leftover food that one might take home from a restaurant. The origin of the phrase comes from the practice of people taking home leftovers for their pets, specifically dogs, which is where it gets its name. The expression is thought to have originated in the United States in the 1940s, during World War II, as a way to reduce food waste. It is believed that it first started at various restaurants across the nation, with some providing waxed paper bags for customers to take home leftovers for their dogs. Another story claims it originated in a New York restaurant called *Dan Stampler's Steak Joint* in 1949, where the owner created a bag with a picture of his Scottish terrier on it and called it a doggie bag.

17. A sandwich short of a picnic

The phrase "a sandwich short of a picnic" is used to refer to someone who is a little eccentric or is not quite right in the head. The expression suggests that the person is missing something essential, just like a sandwich is an essential component of a picnic, but not having one doesn't make a picnic incomplete. The origins of this idiom are fairly recent, the first documented use of it is from the BBC's Lenny Henry Christmas Special, December 1987. It's likely that the phrase was created by the writer as a humorous way to describe someone who is a bit scatterbrained or disoriented. It's commonly used in a light-hearted way, and it's not meant to be taken seriously or as an insult.

18. Right off the bat

The idiom "right off the bat" means immediately or without delay and hesitation. It originated from the American game of baseball, where it is used to describe a well-struck ball. The term was first used in the 1880s, with both literal and figurative usage. It is primarily used in North America, although some believe there may be a link to the game of cricket as well. The earliest written use of this phrase dates back to the early 20th century in a book called *The American Language* by H.L. Mencken, which was published in 1919.

19. On thin ice

The expression "on thin ice" refers to a situation in which someone is in a vulnerable or precarious position. It is thought to have originated in the 16th century and is likely derived from the idea of walking on thin ice, which can be dangerous because it is prone to breaking. It can be used to describe a wide range of situations, including in casual conversation, in written media, or in other forms of communication. The phrase is a common idiom in English and is often used to convey a sense of risk or danger.

20. Smell a rat

The idiom "to smell a rat" means to suspect that something is wrong or that someone is hiding a secret. It is frequently used to express suspicion or distrust of a situation or person. The origin of this phrase is believed to come from the old English saying "to smell rat," which was used to describe the ability of a rat-catcher's dog to detect the presence of rats. The expression was first used in the 1500s to describe the dog's sense of smell to detect rats, then it passed on to be used metaphorically to refer to the ability of humans to sense when something is not right.

Did You Know?

The shortest war in history was between Britain and Zanzibar on August 27, 1896. The conflict lasted just thirty-eight minutes, with the British side quickly gaining control of the East African island-state. This brief conflict marked the end of the Sultanate of Zanzibar and the start of British rule, which lasted until 1964.

The tallest person in history was Robert Wadlow, who was 8 feet 11 inches (2.71 meters) tall.

The highest mountain in the solar system is Olympus Mons, which is located on Mars. It is approximately three times higher than Mount Everest and is the largest volcano in the solar system.

The oldest known tree in the world is a bristlecone pine tree in California's White Mountains. It is over five thousand years old and is still alive.

The longest animal in the world is the lion's mane jellyfish, which can grow up to 120 feet (36.57 meters) in length.

The world's largest snowflake on record was reported to have fallen in Montana in 1887. It was fifteen inches wide and eight inches thick (thirty-eight centimeters wide and twenty centimeters thick).

21. Low man on the totem pole

The expression "low man on the totem pole" is a colloquialism that pertains to an individual occupying the lowest rank within a hierarchy or organization, often characterized by a lack of power or authority. This phrase is frequently used to describe a newcomer to a job or organization, or an individual who is not held in high esteem. It originated from North American indigenous cultures, specifically from the totem poles found in many tribes. Totem poles are wooden sculptures that depict the tribe's history, legends, and spiritual beliefs, with figures arranged in a hierarchical order, with the most significant figures at the top and the less significant figures at the bottom. The phrase was first used in the early 20th century and was coined by Fred Allen, an American comedian, in the 1940s.

22. Up in arms

"Up in arms" has been in use since the 16th century and originally referred to a physical posture in which a person held their arms up in a defensive or aggressive position, often in preparation for battle. The phrase has evolved over time to take on a more figurative meaning, and is now commonly used to refer to a situation in which a group of people are strongly and actively protesting or opposing something. The exact origin of the expression is uncertain, but it likely developed from the literal practice of soldiers raising their weapons in preparation for combat. The phrase has been used in a variety of contexts over the centuries, including in political and social protests, and is now a common idiom in English. In modern usage, it typically refers to a situation in which a group of people are strongly and actively opposing or protesting against something.

23. Full of beans

"Full of beans" is a colloquial phrase that is used to express the state of being lively, energetic, and enthusiastic. It is often used to describe someone who is in a good mood, talkative, or active. The origins of this expression are not entirely clear, but it is believed to have emerged in Europe in the 14th century. According to one theory, the idiom has its origins in the practice of feeding horses exclusively with beans grown for animal feed. The consumption of these beans was observed to result in a noticeable increase in the horses' liveliness and energy, leading to the coining of the phrase to describe this state of vivacity. Another theory is that it comes from the saying "full of life," which has a similar meaning. Additionally, the phrase "full of pep" also carries a similar connotation. It is worth noting that this idiom is not limited to describing positive characteristics, it can also be used in a negative sense to refer to someone who is overly talkative or excessively active, especially when it is seen as annoying or unwanted.

24. Play by ear

"Playing by ear" is a phrase that refers to a musician's ability to play a piece of music without the need for sheet music. This means that the musician is able to listen to a piece of music, and then replicate it on their instrument without the need for written notation. This skill is often associated with pianists and keyboard players, but it can also apply to other instruments such as guitar, drums, and even singing. The origins of the expression date back to the 18th century, when musicians were primarily self-taught. In this era, written music was not as widely available as it is today, and many musicians had to rely on their own ability to replicate what they heard. Over time, the idiom "play by ear" has come to be used more broadly to mean improvising or going with the flow without a specific plan or script.

25. Crème de la crème

The idiom "crème de la crème" is a French phrase that literally means "cream of the cream" and is used to describe the best of the best, the elite, or the top of a group or class. The origin of this expression is thought to come from the culinary world, where it was used to refer to the finest and most expensive ingredients, like the cream that rises to the top of the milk. The idiom originated in France, where items like cream and cheese have been popular for centuries and are considered symbols of elegance and exclusivity. People who had cream or cream-based desserts in their homes would have been considered wealthy.

26. An eye for an eye

"An eye for an eye" is a principle of retaliation in which the punishment inflicted on an offender is equivalent to the harm suffered by the victim. It is frequently used to refer to the idea of seeking revenge or retribution for a wrongdoing. The phrase comes from ancient Mesopotamian and Hebrew cultures, and is found in the Code of Hammurabi and the Hebrew Bible, both dating back to around 1750 BC. The principle of "an eye for an eye" was intended to limit retaliation and ensure that the punishment fit the crime, rather than allowing for excessive or arbitrary punishment. This concept was later adopted by other ancient cultures, such as the Greeks and Romans, and has been a part of legal systems and cultures around the world.

27. Stick one's neck out

The expression "stick one's neck out" describes taking a risk or making a bold move, often in a situation where there is a potential for failure or negative consequences. The phrase is derived from the image of a turtle or other animal sticking its neck out of its shell, which would be a vulnerable position as it exposes its neck to attack. By extension, the idiom is used to refer to someone who is taking a risk or putting themselves in a potentially dangerous or vulnerable position by speaking out or taking action. Another idea suggests that the phrase may have originated as American slang some sixty years ago, based on the backyard chicken that was laid on a chopping block with its neck stretched out, ready to be beheaded with an ax. This theory suggests that the saying means to take a risk and expose oneself to criticism, which is closely related to an older form of the phrase that can be found in Shakespeare's play *Henry V*, where Fluellen says, "Let his neck answer for it."

28. Touch base

The phrase "touch base" is used to describe the act of making contact or having a brief conversation with someone, usually for the purpose of catching up or checking in. This terminology comes from the world of sports, specifically baseball in America. In baseball, touching bases as a batter rounds the infield is necessary in order to advance. The expression was adopted into everyday language in the 1930s and is one of many baseball-related idioms that have been incorporated into everyday language. For example, "getting to first base" means to make a positive start, "off base" means to be mistaken or wide of the mark, and "touching all the bases" means to have everything covered and implies success, similar to hitting a home run and touching all the bases in a victory circuit.

29. New ground

The expression "new ground" or "to break new ground" is a phrase that has been in use for centuries. It originates from the literal act of breaking new ground in agriculture or construction, where new land is being cleared or worked on for the first time. The term has been used throughout history in diverse areas, including mining, excavating, farming, archaeology, arboriculture, and even animal training. The idiom has become popularized in its current context due to its versatility and wide range of usage. It implies that something is different, innovative, or original, and it could also imply that the new thing being done is taking a new direction or is a first-time attempt.

30. Hold the fort

The phrase "hold the fort" originated in the United States during the 1800s along the American Frontier. The expression is thought to have come from the military, where soldiers were ordered to hold a fort or stronghold against an enemy attack, and it was used as a call to action, urging people to defend their position and not to give up. One example of the origin is traced to an order given by General William Tecumseh Sherman in 1864, which was repeated as, "Hold the fort [against the enemy at Allatoona] at all costs, for I am coming." This phrase was used as a battle cry to remind them of their duty and to not give up.

Did You Know?

The Great Wall of China is a series of fortifications made of brick, tamped earth, stone, and other materials, generally built along an east-to-west line across the northern borders of China to protect against the raids and invasions of various nomadic tribes throughout China's history. It is the longest wall in the world, stretching over thirteen thousand miles (20,900 kilometers) and is a **UNESCO** World Heritage Site.

A blue whale is the largest animal on earth and its heart is accordingly massive. In fact, a blue whale's heart is so big that a human could swim through its arteries. It can weigh up to a thousand pounds (454 kilograms) and is around the size of a small car.

The Empire State Building is a world-famous skyscraper located in New York City. It was completed in just one year and forty-five days, with construction starting on March 17, 1930, and the building opening to the public on May 1, 1931. At the time of its completion, it was the tallest building in the world, a title it held for forty years.

A group of flamingos is called a "flamboyance." This term refers to the birds' striking appearance and graceful movements, and is used to describe a gathering of these distinctive, wading birds. Flamingos are known for their long, thin legs and distinctive pink coloration, which comes from the pigments in the algae and small crustaceans that make up their diet.

31. At face value

"At face value" means to accept something as it appears without questioning or examining it further. The phrase suggests that the person is looking only at the surface or exterior of something, rather than examining it more deeply. It is commonly used to describe someone who is too trusting or gullible, and who is not skeptical or critical enough when evaluating information. The term "face value" has been used literally since the 1870s to refer to the monetary value printed on a bank note, stock certificate, bond, or ticket. These items may often sell at prices that are higher than the valuation written on them. But, if an item is sold for the amount of money printed on its face, it is said to be sold at face value. The term has been used figuratively since the late 1800s.

32. Swan song

The term "swan song" refers to a final performance or appearance, especially one that is considered to be the best or most memorable. It is frequently used to describe an artist's final work or an athlete's final game. The origins of this idiom can be traced back to the ancient Greek myth of the swan, which was said to sing a beautiful song just before it died. The myth of the swan song was first recorded in the works of the Greek playwright Aeschylus in his play *Agamemnon*, which was written in 458 BC. In the play, Cassandra sings a death-laden lament like a swan before she dies. The myth of the swan song is a well-known motif that was popularized by the Romans and extensively utilized in literature and visual art. The legend states that swans maintain a characteristic silence throughout their lives, only to produce a melodious, final song upon their imminent death. However, it is important to note that this is a misconception, as swans are actually quite vocal creatures and are not known for singing melodic songs.

33. Heart misses a beat

The idiom "heart misses a beat" means to experience a sudden feeling of excitement or surprise. The origin of this saying is related to the physical sensation of the heart skipping a beat or pausing briefly in response to some sort of stimulation or excitement. The earliest written use of this phrase dates back to the early 20th century. It appears in a book called *The American Language* by H.L. Mencken, which was published in 1919. The book includes the line, "To have one's heart miss a beat is to experience a sudden feeling of excitement or surprise."

34. Feel like death warmed up

To "look or feel like death warmed up" is used to describe a person who looks or feels very sick or unwell. It first came about in the United Kingdom in the early 20th century. One theory is that it comes from the idea of death being personified as a cold or pale figure, and that the act of "warming up" death would involve bringing it back to life or giving it some color. Another theory is that it may have originated as a way of describing the appearance of someone who has been ill or has not been taking care of themselves. Nowadays, it's used in a lighthearted or playful manner, implying that the person is not actually on the brink of death but simply looks very ill.

35. Fair dinkum

The phrase "fair dinkum" originated in Australia in the late 19th century. It is derived from the word "dinkum," which is a slang term that has two meanings: "work" and "fair play." The term "dinkum" originated as "honest toil" and was used to refer to hardworking, honest labor. The expression "fair dinkum" is a combination of the word "dinkum" and the adjective "fair," which means "just" or "true." This idiom is used to indicate that something is true or genuine, and also to express agreement.

36. Fish out of water

The idiom "fish out of water" refers to someone who is feeling uncomfortable or out of place in a particular situation or environment. This phrase suggests the idea of a fish being removed from its natural habitat, where it is able to swim and thrive, and placed in an unfamiliar setting where it is unable to function as it normally would. This idiom has a long history, with the first recorded use of it appearing in the work of English writer Geoffrey Chaucer in the year 1483. In his famous book, *The Canterbury Tales*, Chaucer used this expression to describe a character who was struggling to ride a horse and felt uneasy in this new and unfamiliar situation: "... A huge man, uncouth; a master of vessel and knew all the ports; not ride well; like a fish out of water as sat on his horse."

37. Rings a bell

The expression "rings a bell" means to seem familiar or to remind one of something. It is often used when someone cannot quite remember or place something, but it is familiar in some way. There are a few theories about the origins of this idiom, including the idea that it may be a reference to the ringing of a bell to signal the start or end of an event, or to the bell that is rung to signify the start or end of a round in a boxing match. One proposed explanation for the origin of this idiomatic expression is its association with the research of Ivan Pavlov, a late 19th and early 20th century Russian physiologist and neurologist. In his groundbreaking study, Pavlov demonstrated the phenomenon of classical conditioning in dogs through the use of a ringing bell as a conditioned stimulus. The dogs, having consistently received food in conjunction with the sound of the bell, eventually exhibited a conditioned response of salivation at the mere auditory cue of the bell, anticipating the presentation of food.

38. Get out of hand

To "get out of hand" means to become difficult to control or manage. It is often used to refer to a situation or event that has become chaotic or unmanageable. The phrase is thought to have originated in the early 20th century and it's likely derived from the idea of trying to hold onto something and losing control of it. The expression comes from the concept of losing control of a horse when riding a team of horses pulling a wagon. If the rider lets go of the reins or does not keep a firm grip, then they cannot control the horses. Hence, the horses will be "out of hand."

39. Go back to the drawing board

The idiom "go back to the drawing board" means to start something again from the beginning or to go back to the planning stage. It is mainly used in the context of business or engineering, when a project or product is not successful and needs to be redesigned or reevaluated. The origin of this idiom is thought to come from the practice of using a drawing board in design and engineering. A drawing board is a large, flat surface used to make and modify technical drawings. When a project or product is not successful, designers or engineers might have to go back to the drawing board and start again from the beginning, redesigning and reevaluating their plans. The phrase was first seen in a cartoon by the US cartoonist Peter Arno, which was published in *The New Yorker* in 1941. The cartoon shows a smoldering airplane that has just crashed and a designer is walking away saying, "Well, back to the old drawing board."

40. Sleep with the fishes

To "sleep with the fishes" is a phrase that is used to refer to death, particularly murder. It may have been used by the Mafia and other criminal organizations to describe disposing of someone's body by throwing it in the ocean, where it would "sleep with the fishes." This expression was popularized by movies and TV shows that depicted the American Mafia, such as *The Godfather* and *The Sopranos*. However, the origin of the idiom may go back much farther. According to some theories, the phrase was used by Edmund Spencer in the 1830s in *Sketches of Germany and the Germans*, where he described a trip by a British angler to an area occupied by superstitious villagers who considered fly fishing a form of black magic. Spencer wrote: "This terrible apprehension was soon circulated from village to village: the deluded peasants broke in pieces the pretty painted magic wand, and forcibly put to flight the magician himself, vowing, with imprecations, if he repeated his visit, they would send him to sleep with the fishes." Even in

Homer's *The Iliad*, there is a passage, "Make your bed with the fishes now..."

Did You Know?

A sneeze can travel up to a hundred miles (160 kilometres) per hour and can spread germs up to twenty feet (six meters) away.

A single teaspoon of a neutron star would weigh about six billion tons.

A cat has the ability to always land on its feet thanks to a flexible spine and an inner ear that helps it sense which way is up.

The average person spends six months of their life waiting for red lights to turn green.

The Nile is the longest river in the world, stretching over four thousand miles (6,437 kilometers) from its source in Burundi to its mouth in Egypt. The river has been a vital source of water and transportation for the people of Egypt for thousands of years and played a key role in the development of ancient Egyptian civilization. The Nile remains an important economic resource for the countries through which it flows, providing water for agriculture, industry, and human consumption.

The air you exhale contains enough carbon dioxide to kill a person if it were all concentrated in one place. This is because carbon dioxide is toxic in high concentrations. Normal levels of carbon dioxide in the air we breathe are harmless, but if the concentration becomes too high, it can interfere with oxygen uptake in the lungs and lead to suffocation. This is why miners and underwater divers often use breathing apparatus that filters out excess carbon dioxide to keep air supply safe.

41. Skid row

"Skid row" is a term used to describe a run-down and poor neighborhood in a city. It's often where homeless people or people who move around a lot live. The phrase started in the late 1800s when loggers would set up camp near the "skid road" where they slid logs to the sawmill or river. Over time, the areas became known as "skid row." During the Great Depression, many people lost their jobs and became homeless. This led to the creation of skid row areas in cities all over the US. These places were known for having a lot of homeless people and cheap places to stay. They were often poor, had crime, and made people feel hopeless. Today, skid row areas still exist in many US cities, with an area in downtown Los Angeles functionally termed Skid Row. The term "skid row" has also come to describe communities of people who struggle with addiction or mental health problems. People are trying to make these areas better by improving housing and offering more help to those in need.

42. Hard pill to swallow

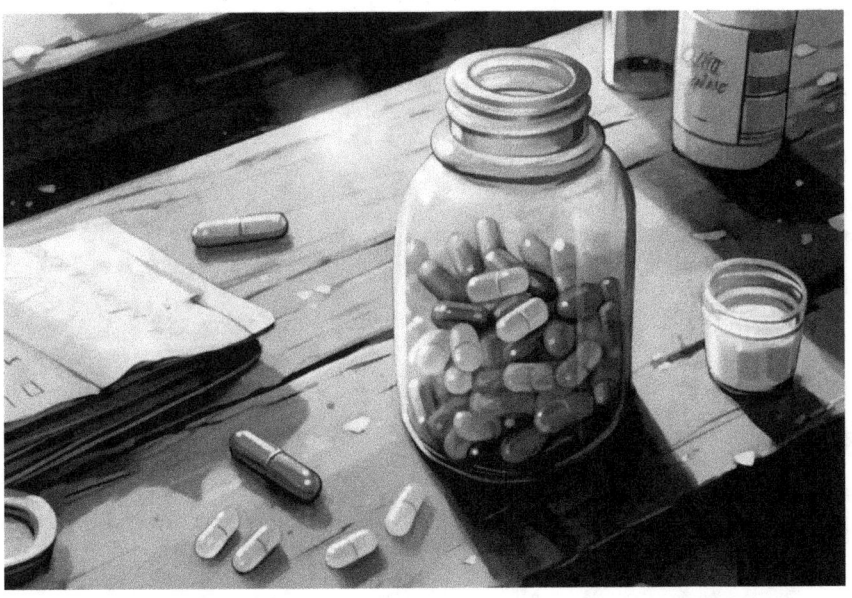

A "hard pill to swallow" is used to describe something that is difficult to accept or believe, or that is painful to endure. It is one variant of an idiom that has been in use for hundreds of years. The expression first appeared in the 1600s as a "pill to swallow" and, at the time, a pill was considered a foul thing to ingest. The variation "a bitter pill to swallow" came into use in the 1700s, and the final expression, "a hard pill to swallow," came into use in the 1800s. Nowadays, the phrase "a bitter pill to swallow" is about twice as popular as the term "a hard pill to swallow." This expression in its current form started appearing in written work, with the earliest use of this idiom found in the *Morning Journal* newspaper from 1829: "That they will prove a hard pill for Turkey to swallow is to be expected, unless, indeed, some decided friend has recently sprung up, who will not allow Turkey to be so crippled as to make her fall an easy prey next time she is attacked."

43. No brainer

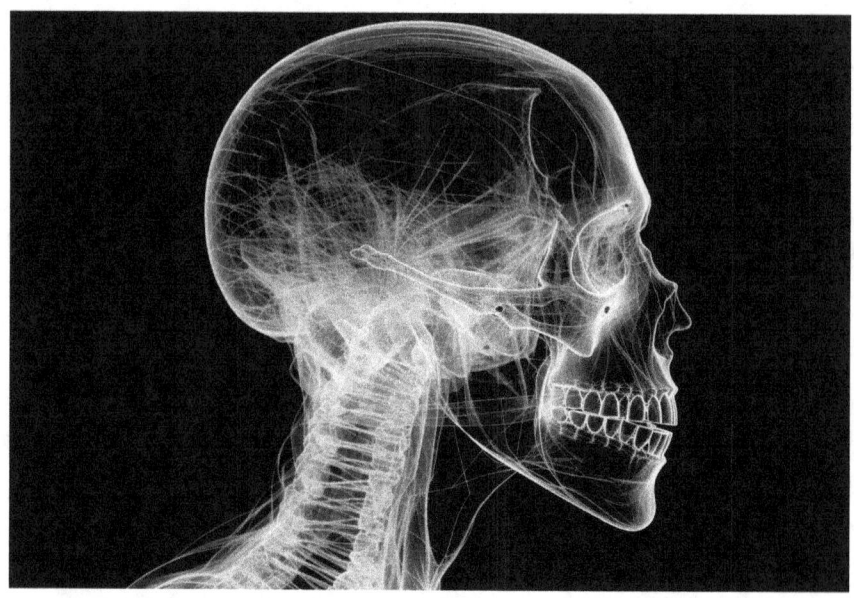

The term "no brainer" is used to describe a decision that is very easy to make or a situation that is readily resolved. It originated in the United States in the 1970s and comes from the idea of using one's brain to make decisions or solve problems. The phrase suggests that the decision or situation in question is so obvious or straightforward that it requires little or no thought or effort to make or resolve. Today, it's used in a casual or lighthearted manner, implying that the decision or situation is not particularly important or significant.

44. Chip off the old block

The expression "chip off the old block" refers to a person who closely resembles their parent or other family member in terms of their appearance, personality, or other characteristics. It originated in the 19th century and is likely derived from the idea of carving a small piece or "chip" from a larger block of wood or stone in order to create a new piece that closely resembles the original. Today, the phrase is used to convey a sense of similarity, with the implication that the offspring is just like the parent.

45. Stuck in a rut

To be "stuck in a rut" means that someone is trapped in a situation where they cannot make progress or change. They could feel confined or unfulfilled and may be experiencing a lack of motivation or a sense of stagnation. The idiom goes back to the 1800s when wagons would get stuck in the trenches created by other wagons' wheels on frequently-traveled roads. If one wagon needed to veer off the road, they would frequently find themselves stuck. Nowadays, "stuck in a rut" is often used to refer to someone feeling trapped in a repetitive or unfulfilling situation and unable to make progress.

46. Knee jerk reaction

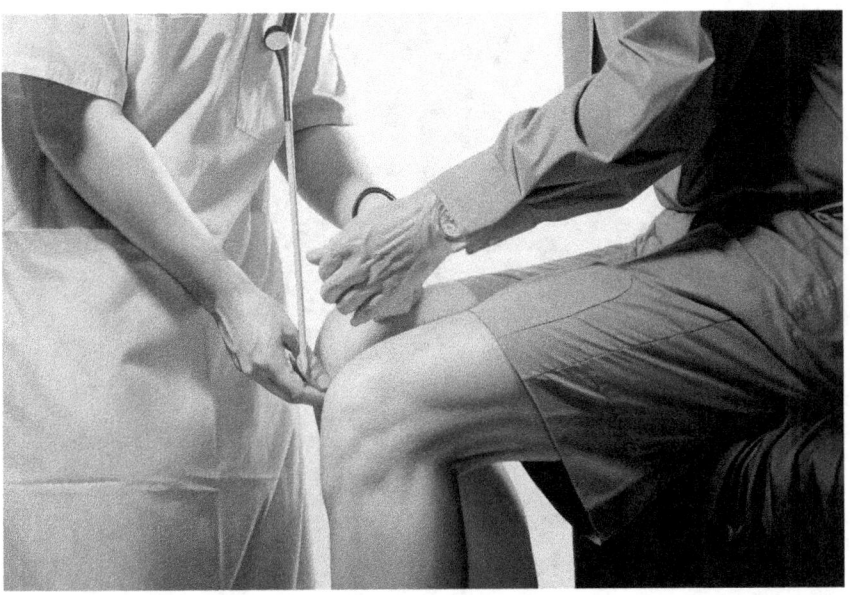

A "knee-jerk reaction" refers to a rapid, automatic, and often emotional response, without careful consideration or thought. It often describes a response that is based on habit, instinct, or preconceived notions, rather than on logical analysis or critical thinking. The origin of this idiom is related to the reflexive action of the knee when the patellar tendon is tapped. When the patellar tendon is tapped, the knee reflexively jerks or kicks outward. This reflex is a simple and automatic response that is controlled by the spinal cord and does not involve conscious thought. The earliest written use of this phrase dates back to the early 20th century. It appears in a book called *Psychology and Life* by Robert S. Woodworth, which was published in 1918. The book defines the term as "a reflex action of the knee caused by a tap on the patellar tendon, and also used to describe a quick and automatic response to something, without careful consideration."

47. Shot across the bow

The phrase "shot across the bow" means a warning or cautionary message. It comes from the naval practice of firing a warning shot across the bow of another ship as a signal to stop or change course. This was a way to avoid a more serious confrontation or conflict at sea. In modern usage, the expression is commonly used to refer to any warning or cautionary message that is meant to prevent a situation from escalating. It can be used in a variety of contexts, such as in business or politics, to signal that further, more serious, action may be taken if necessary.

48. Ground zero

The term "ground zero" is an idiomatic expression that refers to the point of origin or the center of an event or activity, often used in reference to a catastrophic event such as a nuclear explosion, terrorist attack, or natural disaster. The phrase originated in the early 20th century, specifically in reference to the point on the ground directly beneath the point of detonation of a nuclear bomb. The term "ground zero" first came into use on September 4, 1945, in a *New York Times* report on the atomic bombing of Nagasaki, Japan. It was used to describe the location of the bomb's detonation and the area of the most severe damage. It was later used in reference to the point of origin of other catastrophic events, such as the September 11, 2011, terrorist attacks on the World Trade Center in New York City.

49. Packed like sardines

The expression "packed like sardines" describes a situation where people or objects are crowded together in a tight or cramped space. It originated in the early 20th century and comes from the practice of packing sardines in cans. Sardines are small fish that are often packed tightly, one on top of the other, in order to conserve space and make them easier to transport. The image of sardines packed closely together in a can is used as a metaphor for people or objects that are crowded together in a tight or cramped space. The first recorded use of the phrase in print is from the year 1908, in a book called *The Cruise of the Dry Dock* by T. W. H. Crosland.

50. Best of both worlds

The origin of the phrase "the best of both worlds" is unclear, but it has been part of the English language since the late 1800s. The earliest known usage of the expression can be traced back to the novel *Westward Ho!* by the English writer and clergyman Charles Kingsley, published in 1855. However, it is believed that the term existed even before that. The idiom has religious undertones that refer to the two worlds of life and afterlife. In this context, it suggests that a person who leads a virtuous life, and does good deeds for others, will be able to enjoy the fruits of their labor both in this life and in the next. Another theory is that the idiom originated from philosophy, where the idea of having the best of both worlds is achieved by balancing different opposing ideas or beliefs. The phrase became popular in the mid and late 1900s. Despite the uncertainty of its origin, it is commonly understood to mean having the best of two different options without having to choose between them.

Did You Know?

Humans share fifty percent of their DNA with bananas. This fact is due to the similarities in the genetic code of all living things. While it may seem surprising, it's actually a result of the fact that all living things share a common ancestry and have evolved from a single, ancestral organism over billions of years. The similarities in genetic code between species can reveal important information about the relationships between species and the evolutionary processes that have shaped the diversity of life on Earth.

A hummingbird is capable of hovering in midair by flapping its wings at rates of up to eighty beats per second. This remarkable feat of flight is possible due to the high wing-flapping frequency, which generates lift and allows the bird to remain stationary in midair. Hummingbirds are also able to fly forwards, backwards, and even upside down, making them one of the most agile birds in the world.

The human nose can detect over one trillion different scents, making it one of the most advanced sensory organs in the animal kingdom. This incredible ability to distinguish between different scents is due to the complex structure of the olfactory system in the human nose, which contains over four hundred different types of odor receptors. These receptors allow us to detect a wide range of different scents, from the pleasing aroma of freshly baked bread to the unpleasant odor of a skunk. The ability to detect and distinguish between different scents is critical to our survival, as it helps us to identify potential dangers and locate food.

51. Lose your marbles

To "lose your marbles" refers to a situation in which someone becomes confused, irrational, or mentally unstable. It originated in the mid-20th century and is derived from the idea of losing actual marbles, which were small glass or ceramic balls that could roll off and become lost. The phrase is a common idiom in English and is often used to convey a sense of disorientation. It could be put mildly in conversation, as a self-deprecating comment about oneself or in a more severe context of mental illness.

52. Eager beaver

An "eager beaver" describes a person who is enthusiastic, hardworking, and eager to get things done. The phrase is thought to have originated in the United States in the early 20th century, specifically during World War I, where it was used to describe the very eager recruits who were willing to do anything to impress their commanding officers. The origin of the phrase comes from the idea of a beaver, which is a hardworking and industrious animal. Beavers are large rodents that are well known for their skill of building dams that are very large compared to their size. It's important to note that this term is commonly used in a positive way to refer to someone who is hardworking and enthusiastic, but it can also be used in a negative way to describe someone who is overly eager and can be perceived as pushy or impatient.

53. This ain't my first rodeo

"This ain't my first rodeo" is a colloquial phrase that is used to express the speaker's experience and competence in a particular situation. The term means that the speaker is not a novice and has dealt with similar situations before, and is not easily surprised or flustered. The idiom is frequently used to assert one's superiority when a less experienced person is trying to give advice to the more experienced person. The word "ain't" is a slang contraction for "it is not" and the word "rodeo" refers to a contest where cowboys and cowgirls exhibit their skills in various events such as bull riding, bronco riding, and calf roping. The idiom "this ain't my first rodeo" is generally traced back to the movie *Mommie Dearest*.

54. Fifth wheel

The term "fifth wheel" has its origins in the early days of horse-drawn vehicles, specifically wagons and carriages. These vehicles often had four wheels and a central hub on which the fifth wheel was mounted. This fifth wheel served as a support for the vehicle, allowing it to turn more smoothly and easily. However, when a fifth wheel was not needed, it was considered to be an unnecessary addition and a hindrance. The phrase is now used to describe someone or something that is not needed or unnecessary in a situation, often referring to a person who is not part of a group or project and is considered to be an outsider. The term was first recorded in the early 1800s.

55. Cut corners

To "cut corners" refers to taking shortcuts or doing things in a less thorough or efficient manner in order to save money or time and is used to convey a sense of laziness or a lack of attention to detail. It is believed to have originated in the 19th century and likely developed from the literal practice of cutting corners when taking a shortcut or making a journey. In this context, the phrase refers to the idea of taking a shorter or more direct route, often at the expense of efficiency or thoroughness. Now, the expression is used more broadly to describe any situation in which someone takes shortcuts to save time or money.

56. Bear a grudge

To "bear a grudge" means that someone continues to harbor resentment or anger towards someone else, often over a perceived slight that was done to them. It originated from old English in the 16th century and is derived from the idea of bearing or carrying a burden, in this case a negative feeling or emotion. Today, the phrase is mostly used to convey a sense of bitterness or resentment.

57. Chasing rainbows

"Chasing rainbows" refers to the pursuit of something that is unattainable or unlikely to be achieved. It is often used to describe the pursuit of dreams or goals that are unrealistic to attain or to suggest that someone is wasting their time or energy on something that will not bring them any tangible results. The origin of this phrase is likely derived from the phenomenon of a rainbow, which is an optical illusion caused by the refraction of light through water droplets. Rainbows are often seen as symbols of hope and promise, but they are also transient and elusive, and it is impossible to reach or touch one. The idea of chasing something that is fleeting and unattainable is what gives this expression its meaning.

58. Down for the count

The idiom "down for the count" refers to a situation in which someone is unable to continue with a particular activity or task, often due to injury, illness, or exhaustion. It originated in the early 20th century and is derived from the sport of boxing, in which a fighter is considered to be "down for the count" if they are knocked down to the ground and unable to get up within a certain amount of time (usually as long as it takes the referee to count to ten). In modern time, the phrase is used to convey a sense of defeat or incapacity.

59. Hop, skip, and jump

The phrase "hop, skip, and a jump" has its roots in the world of dance, first appearing in the early 1700s as "hop, step, and jump." It referred to a specific sequence of movements in a dance routine. However, by the mid 1700s, the term had evolved to "hop, skip, and a jump," while still referring to a dance move. It wasn't until the early to mid 1800s that the expression began to take on its current meaning of describing a short distance. The idea is that if a destination is just a "hop, skip, and jump" away then it is close by and wouldn't take long to travel to.

60. In hot water

The idiomatic expression "in hot water" refers to a state of trouble or adversity. This phrase has roots that can be traced back to the 17th century and is evocative of being immersed in water that is of such a high temperature as to cause burning. The act of pouring boiling water on intruders or foes was a widespread practice in ancient times, serving as a form of defense or punishment. This was executed from an elevated position, such as an upper-floor window or castle rampart, and was intended to force the unwanted visitors to retreat. The experience of being doused with boiling water would have been a harrowing one.

Did You Know?

The tongue is the only muscle in the human body that is attached at only one end. This makes it unique among all the other muscles in the body, which are attached at both ends and work in pairs to produce movement. The tongue is responsible for various functions, including speaking, swallowing, and tasting. It is also a very strong and flexible muscle that can move in various directions to help us eat and form words.

There are more possible iterations of a game of chess than there are atoms in the observable universe. Chess is a complex game with a large number of possible moves and outcomes, making it difficult to calculate the exact number of iterations. However, it is estimated that there are over 10^{120} possible combinations of moves in a game of chess. This is an astronomical number and far larger than the estimated number of atoms in the observable universe, which is estimated to be around 10^{80}.

The Great Pyramid of Giza, one of the Seven Wonders of the World, is estimated to weigh around six million tons. It was built over 4,500 years ago and is one of the most impressive structures ever created by humans. It is made up of over two million blocks of granite and limestone, each weighing an average of two and a half tons. The sheer size and weight of the pyramid is amazing and it is a testament to the engineering and architectural skills of the ancient Egyptians.

61. Rose-colored glasses

The expression "rose-colored glasses" refers to a tendency to view things in an overly positive or optimistic light. The phrase has been in use since 1861, as recorded in *Tom Brown at Oxford* where it is described as an attitude of cheerful optimism of seeing everything in an attractive, pleasant light. Although the term is often used to describe someone who is unwilling to see the negative aspects of a situation or person, it is also acknowledged that everyone wears these "spectacles" of optimism occasionally. The renowned French singer and songwriter Edith Piaf wrote and sang a song called "La vie en rose," which is the French equivalent of the phrase "rose-colored glasses," and further emphasizes the connection between the idiom and the idea of seeing the world through a positive and optimistic lens.

62. On the ball

"On the ball" is a colloquial expression that suggests a person is alert, ready, and well-informed. The phrase is frequently used to indicate that someone is paying close attention to the current situation and is able to respond quickly and effectively. It can also convey the idea that a person is well-organized and able to manage multiple tasks simultaneously. The term has its origins in sports, specifically in games that involve a ball. The idiom is derived from the earlier expression "keep your eye on the ball," which is a piece of advice that has been given to players of various ball games such as cricket, golf, croquet, and baseball. The phrase is found in early records of these sports and many people believe that baseball is the source of this idiomatic expression.

63. Yada yada

"Yada yada" is a colloquial term that denotes the act of succinctly summarizing or skipping over a lengthy or insignificant conversation or action. The phrase is believed to have originated in vaudeville (a theatrical genre of entertainment born in France at the end of the 19th century), with the spelling "yaddeyahdah" being used by Lenny Bruce, an American comedian active in the 1960s. The resurgence of popularity of the expression can be attributed to the "Seinfeld" television series, and it is often rendered with three "yadas" rather than two. People usually use "yada yada" in casual conversation as a way of skipping over unimportant or uninteresting details.

64. On cloud nine

The expression "on cloud nine" refers to a state of extreme happiness. It originated from the phrase "in cloud-cuckoo-land," which was used to describe a state of being out of touch with reality or disconnected from the world. The term "on cloud nine" is now used to describe a state of contentment and often conveys a sense of being in a dream-like state or being disconnected from the everyday world. It's applicable in a wide range of situations, including happiness in romantic relationships, career successes, and other events or experiences that bring great joy or fulfillment.

65. Spin doctor

The term "spin doctor" is used to describe a person who is skilled at manipulating or shaping public opinion or perception, often in a way that is misleading or deceptive. It originated in the United Kingdom in the 1980s and it comes from the idea of spinning, or twisting, the truth or facts in order to present a particular point of view or interpretation. It is often employed in a negative or critical way, implying that the person is engaging in unethical or dishonest behavior; however, it can also be used more generally to describe any person who is skilled at manipulating or changing public opinion, regardless of their intentions or motivations.

66. Foaming at the mouth

The phrase "foaming at the mouth" is used to describe a person who is extremely angry or agitated. Its origins can be traced back to the medical condition known as rabies. Rabies is a viral disease that affects the nervous system of warm-blooded animals, including humans. One of the most common symptoms of rabies is excessive salivation, which leads to the production of foam or froth around the animal's mouth. This symptom has been observed since ancient times, as described in the texts of Hippocrates and Galen. The appearance of animals affected with rabies, in which they literally foam at the mouth while in a blind stupor that can include attacks that look like they stem from anger or rage, is the origin of the term.

67. A left handed compliment

The idiom "a left-handed compliment" refers to a remark or compliment that is meant to be complimentary but is actually insincere, derogatory, or has a sarcastic meaning. The origin is thought to be related to the idea of a left-handed compliment being "backhanded." The earliest written use of this phrase dates back to the late 19th century. It appears in a book called *The Man with Two Left Feet* by P.G. Wodehouse, which was published in 1917. The book includes the line, "It was one of those left-handed compliments that are more offensive than open abuse."

68. Fool's errand

The term "fool's errand" means a useless or pointless pursuit. It often describes something that is a waste of time or effort, and is unlikely to achieve any worthwhile result. The origin of this idiom is thought to be related to the idea of a fool or someone who is not very intelligent or capable. The earliest written use of this phrase dates back to the 16th century. It appears in a book called *The Proverbs, Epigrams, and Miscellanies* by John Heywood, which was published in 1562. The book includes the line, "Send not a boy on a man's errand, nor a fool on any errand."

69. On his last legs

The idiom "on his last legs" means to be near the end or close to failing or collapsing. It suggests that the person or thing in question is in a weakened state and may not be able to continue for much longer. There are a few possible origins for this phrase, including the idea of a person or animal being near the end of their physical or mental endurance and being unable to walk on their legs any longer, or the idea of a person or thing being in a weakened state, and being at risk of failing or collapsing. It is often used to suggest that the person or thing in question is in a precarious state and that it may not be able to continue for much longer.

70. Shotgun wedding

A "shotgun wedding" refers to a wedding that takes place under pressure or coercion, often due to an unplanned pregnancy. It often encompasses a situation where one or both parties are forced into marriage due to societal or familial expectations. The origin of the phrase can be traced back to the 19th century in the United States, from the practice of using a shotgun to intimidate the man into marrying the woman with whom he had gotten pregnant.

Did You Know?

Vatican City, officially called the Holy See, is a tiny city-state located in the heart of Rome, Italy. It is the smallest independent state in the world by both area and population. It is the headquarters of the Roman Catholic Church and the residence of the Pope, making it a major center of pilgrimage for millions of Catholics worldwide.

The human lung has a surface area of about 753 square feet (seventy square meters), which is roughly equivalent to the size of a tennis court. This large surface area allows for efficient gas exchange between the lungs and the bloodstream, which is crucial for breathing and getting oxygen to the body's cells. The lungs are also responsible for removing waste gases like carbon dioxide from the bloodstream, ensuring that the body's internal environment remains healthy.

The human body can survive without food for approximately one month, but without water, survival is limited to only one week or less. Water is an essential component in maintaining balance in the body's various functions and performing crucial processes, such as digestion, transportation of nutrients, regulation of body temperature, and elimination of waste. The human body consists of 50-75% water and even small decreases in hydration levels can result in serious consequences such as fatigue, headaches, dry mouth, dizziness, and in severe cases, unconsciousness or death. The time an individual can survive without water varies based on factors such as age, health, climate, and physical activity levels, with an average of three to five days for an adult. It is important to consume sufficient amounts of water daily, with a recommended intake of eight glasses or half a gallon (two liters), although individual needs may vary.

71. In the fast lane

The phrase "in the fast lane" refers to a situation in which a person is moving or working at a fast pace, usually in a way that is intense or highly focused. It can also refer to a lifestyle or mindset that is characterized by fast-paced activity and a desire for success or achievement. The expression is often used to describe someone who is ambitious and driven, and who is always looking for new challenges or opportunities. The term is frequently employed in a positive way to praise someone's hard work and determination, but it can also be used in a negative way to suggest that someone is overburdened or overwhelmed by their busy schedule. The idiom emerged in the mid-20th century and was influenced by the metaphor of a highway or roadway with different lanes for different speeds. In this context, the "fast lane" would be the lane on the highway that is reserved for the fastest-moving traffic. The phrase may also have been influenced by the idea of "fast living," or a lifestyle that is characterized by fast-paced activity and a desire for success or achievement.

72. Fortune favors the bold

"Fortune favors the bold" is an idiomatic expression that means that people who take risks and are bold are more likely to be successful than those who are timid and hesitant. The origin of this expression can be traced back to ancient literature, specifically to the play titled *Phormio* by Roman playwright Terence in 161 BC, where the proverbial phrase "Fortis fortuna adiuvat" was used in Act 1, which means "fortune helps the brave." However, it's not the literal English translation of what Terence wrote. Later, the Roman poet Virgil used the phrase better in his epic poem *Aeneid*, saying "audentes Fortuna iuvat" which translates to "Fortune favors the bold," where "Fortuna" is the name of the goddess of luck. There are several other versions of the term such as "fortune favors the brave," "fate favors the bold," "God favors the bold," "those who are willing to take a risk are often highly rewarded," and "bravery is oftentimes rewarded."

73. Looking to your laurels

The idiom "looking to your laurels" refers to a situation where steps are being taken to maintain or improve one's position or reputation, especially in relation to others who are competing or striving for similar goals. It originated in the 19th century and is derived from the ancient Greek tradition of awarding laurel wreaths to victors and other accomplished individuals as a symbol of honor and achievement. Nowadays, the phrase is mainly used to convey a sense of ambition or determination.

74. You can't judge a book by its cover

"You can't judge a book by its cover" is a way of saying that one should not look at the superficial characteristics of a person or object and make over-arching judgments. The origin of this phrase is from a 1944 edition of the journal *American Speech*, where it first appeared in the form "You can't judge a book by its binding." The phrase was popularized even more when it appeared in the 1946 murder mystery *Murder in the Glass Room* by Edwin Rolfe and Lester Fuller.

75. Big fish in a small pond

The phrase "big fish in a small pond" is frequently used to describe someone who has achieved a high level of status or accomplishment within a specific community or environment, but who may not have the same level of success or recognition in a larger, more competitive setting. The expression originated in the early 20th century and was used in the context of business or politics. It's inspired by the idea that a large fish will dominate a small body of water, but may struggle to compete in a bigger, tougher environment. In modern usage, the idiom is often employed to acknowledge or praise someone for their accomplishments within a specific context, while also suggesting that they may face challenges or setbacks if they try to expand their influence or success to a wider audience.

76. Pipe down

"Pipe down" is an expression that is used to tell someone to be quiet or stop talking. It originated in the 19th century in the context of ships at sea. In naval ships, pipes or whistles were used to signal different orders to the crew. When the order to "pipe down" was given, it meant that the crew should stop making noise and be quiet. Similarly, "pipe up" is an idiom that is used to tell someone to speak up or to speak louder. It originated from naval ships as well and when the order to "pipe up" was given, it meant that the crew should speak up and be heard. The context and the tone of the speaker are important to determine the correct meaning of the phrase.

77. Ins and outs

Geoffrey Chaucer, an English poet, first used the phrase "ins and outs" in his poem *Troilus and Criseyde* in the late 1300s. The term was used again within the political sphere in 1814 in the writings of Thomas Jefferson to describe two opposing political parties; the party in power was "in," and the opposing party was "out." Only in the 19th century did the idiom begin being used in the way we know it now. Nowadays, the phrase has a broader application, referring to the details or specifics of something, particularly its intricate or complex aspects. It is often used to express a thorough or complete understanding of something, including the small details or nuances.

78. To move at a snail's pace

"To move at a snail's pace" means to move very slowly or to progress very little. The phrase is commonly utilized to describe a situation that is taking a long time to develop or to describe someone who is working at a very slow speed. The expression is a metaphor, comparing the movement of a person or thing to that of a snail, which is known for its slow pace of movement. The origin of the idiom can be traced back to Shakespeare's play, *Richard III*, spoken by King Richard in act 4, scene 3, where he says, "Delay leads impotent and snail-paced beggary."

79. Go cold turkey

The idiom "go cold turkey" means to stop using something suddenly and completely, especially a habit or addiction. It is often used in the context of quitting a habit such as smoking or drug use, and often implies the physical symptoms of withdrawal that may occur when someone stops using a substance abruptly. The origins of this expression are not entirely clear, but it is thought to have originated in the United States in the mid-20th century. One theory is that it refers to the goosebumps and "cold" skin that can occur during withdrawal from some substances, while another theory suggests that it may be a reference to the phrase "cold feet," which is used to describe someone who is having second thoughts or is reluctant to do something.

80. Burn one's boats

The idiomatic expressions "burn one's bridges" and "burn one's boats" have their origins in both ancient Roman military tactics as well as the story of the Spanish conquistador Hernán Cortés. The Roman armies would destroy bridges in order to stop the enemy from fleeing and to cut off their supply lines. They would also destroy their boats upon landing on the enemy's shore to eliminate the possibility of retreat, thus forcing them to fight to the death or victory. Similarly, when Cortés landed in Mexico in 1519, he ordered his men to burn their ships as a symbolic gesture to demonstrate to his men that they were now committed to the conquest of the Aztec Empire and that there was no turning back. Both of these historical events gave rise to the use of "burn one's bridges" or "burn one's boats," which are used to describe a situation where someone makes a bold and irreversible decision, such as quitting a job or ending a relationship, in which the individual commits to a course of action with no possibility of turning back.

Did You Know?

A cockroach can live for several weeks without its head due to their ability to breathe through tiny holes in their bodies, rather than their mouths. Cockroaches have a decentralized nervous system, which means that their vital functions are controlled by individual ganglia, or clusters of nerve cells, rather than by a single brain. As a result, a cockroach can continue to move, feed, and even mate for a few weeks after losing its head, until it ultimately succumbs to dehydration.

Sloths are known for their slow-moving and unique lifestyle, and only defecate once a week. They are arboreal mammals that spend the majority of their lives hanging upside down in trees. Sloths have a low metabolism and move slowly to conserve energy, which also makes them excellent at avoiding predators.

An octopus has three hearts, which are essential for pumping blood throughout its eight limbs and complex nervous system. Octopuses are also known for their ability to change color and texture to blend in with their surroundings, making them excellent at camouflage. This helps them evade predators or ambush prey, and they can rapidly change their appearance to match the colors and patterns of their surroundings.

Bats are known for their long lifespan relative to their size, with some species living over twenty years. They are the only mammals that can fly and have unique adaptations that allow them to live for such a long time, including a slow metabolism, low reproductive rate, and the ability to enter into a state of torpor, or reduced activity, during winter months to conserve energy. Bats play an important role in the ecosystem, as many species are pollinators or consume large quantities of insects, making them important for controlling pest populations.

81. Pony up

The term "pony up" means to pay or contribute money, usually in a specific or agreed upon amount. The expression is thought to have originated in the late 19th century and is believed to have come from the practice of using small coins called "ponies" in horse racing bets. However, there is also a theory that the term dates back to the 16th century and comes from the Latin phrase "legem pone" which is found in Psalm 119. This theory suggests that the term originated in Britain, and it was used on the Quarter Day, which is the first payday of the year (this day was March 25th). Although this theory is less common, it is still an explanation for the origin of the phrase "pony up."

82. Face the music

The idiom "face the music" means to accept the consequences of one's actions or to confront a difficult situation or unpleasant reality. It is commonly used to describe the act of taking responsibility and dealing with the consequences, even if they are difficult. The origin of this idiom is not entirely clear, but it might have come from the United States in the mid-19th century. One theory is that it may be a reference to the practice of holding a formal military court martial, where a soldier accused of an offense would be required to stand at attention and listen to the reading of the charges against them. Another theory is that it may be a reference to the practice of facing a firing squad, where a person accused of a crime would be required to stand and face the guns of their executioners. The earliest recorded use of the phrase "face the music" dates back to 1834, when it appeared in *The New Hampshire Statesman & State Journal*.

83. A hairsbreadth

The term "a hairsbreadth" describes an extremely narrow margin or distance. It originated in the United Kingdom in the 16th century and comes from the idea of a hair being thin and slender. The phrase suggests that the margin or distance in question is so small that it is almost imperceptible, similar to the width of a single hair. Today, the idiom is mainly used in a dramatic or suspenseful manner, implying that the margin or distance in question is so small that it could easily be missed or overlooked.

84. You look like a million dollars

"You look like a million dollars" is a compliment used to express that someone looks very attractive or impressive. The origin comes from the early 20th century when a million dollars was considered a large and impressive amount of money. To look like a million dollars was to look wealthy, successful, and put together. It originated in the United States, where the expression of wealth and success was particularly important in the 1920s, a period of great prosperity and social change. The phrase was commonly used in popular culture, such as in movies and songs, and it quickly became a commonly used expression of admiration. The expression has since evolved to be less focused on wealth and more on someone's overall appearance. Today it's used to express admiration for someone's physical appearance, as well as their style, grooming, and general sense of fashion.

85. Green fingers

The term "green fingers" is an expression describing someone who has a natural talent for gardening and cultivating plants. It is often used to portray a person who is skilled at growing flowers, fruits, and vegetables and who is able to make them thrive. The origins of the phrase are not entirely clear, but there are several possible sources. The first hypothesis suggests that it came from the discoloration of a gardener's hands from the exposure to algae and crushed leaves in the course of their work with plants. The second theory associates the term with the "Green Man," an archetypal symbol denoting the growth and vitality of plants in various ancient religious systems. The third theory suggests that it is modeled on the myth of the Midas touch, where a king's touch was said to transmute objects into gold. The expression "green thumb" is primarily the American version of the idiom, while "green fingers" is primarily the British version.

86. Don't give up your day job

"Don't give up your day job" is a sarcastic expression that is used to tell a person that they are not very good at something, especially when they haven't given a serious effort into the attempt. The phrase suggests that they should stick to their regular job, as they are not likely to succeed in the endeavor they are currently undertaking. The earliest recorded instance of this phrase is from a publication called *The Billboard* (Cincinnati, Ohio) on June 16th, 1951, in an article where it was quoted as, "Berle, I caught you on TV. Don't give up the day job."

87. The jury is out

The phrase "the jury is out" is commonly used in situations where there is ongoing debate, uncertainty, or lack of information about a particular issue. It can be applied in a variety of contexts, such as in politics, business, or science, to indicate that a decision or judgment has not yet been made and that more information is needed before a conclusion can be reached. The origin of the expression is traced back to the court system where juries hear cases and make decisions. The jury, made up of citizens, is responsible for listening to the evidence presented by both the prosecution and the defense, and then deliberate in secret to reach a verdict. The jury's decision, also known as the verdict, must be unanimous, meaning that all jurors must agree on the outcome. The jury deliberation is secret, hence the phrase "the jury is out" indicating that no one knows the outcome yet.

88. Game the system

The phrase "game the system" means to use clever tactics or strategies to gain an advantage within a particular system or process. The origins of this term can be traced back to the field of systems engineering in the mid-1970s, where it was used to describe the manipulation of systems to achieve a desired outcome. However, it did not become widely popular in general culture until the 1990s. The expression implies that the person using the tactics is aware of the rules and uses them to their advantage in a clever and cunning way. It is also frequently utilized in a negative way to describe someone who is perceived as manipulating or cheating to get ahead.

89. Hand Over Fist

The origins of the idiom "hand over fist" are unclear, but it may have come about in the mid-19th century. One theory is that the phrase comes from how sailors used to haul in a ship's anchor by pulling on a rope with both hands, making a fist around the rope, and then quickly repeating the motion as they pulled it in. This action would have looked as if the sailors were grabbing the anchor with both hands and collecting it quickly, or "hand over fist." Another theory is that it comes from a person counting their money quickly and efficiently as if they were grabbing it with both hands and counting it rapidly. Regardless of its origins, the idiom is now used to describe someone quickly earning or acquiring something and in large amounts. It suggests that the person is receiving money or other resources at a swift pace, as if they are grabbing them with both hands.

90. Call it a day

The idiom "call it a day" means to stop working or to end a task for the day. The expression began with the phrase "call it half a day," which was originally recorded in 1838. This term was used to refer to employees who went home before the end of the workday and their attendance records would reflect that they had worked a half day. Later, the phrase was transformed into "call it a day," which means that work on that particular day is completely over. The first recorded use of this expression was in 1919.

Did You Know?

The Amazon Rainforest, also known as the Amazon Jungle, is a vast and complex ecosystem that covers over 2.1 million square miles (5.4 square kilometers) and spans across nine countries in South America. It is home to an estimated 390 billion individual trees and thousands of species of plants and animals, many of which are not found anywhere else in the world. The Amazon is also known for its incredible biodiversity, with an estimated ten percent of the world's known species residing within its boundaries. The rainforest also plays a critical role in regulating the world's climate and weather patterns, as it helps to absorb carbon dioxide and release oxygen into the atmosphere.

The Galapagos Islands, located off the coast of Ecuador, are a unique and diverse ecosystem that have long been of interest to scientists and naturalists. The islands are home to a variety of species found nowhere else in the world, including giant tortoises, marine iguanas, and flightless cormorants. The Galapagos Islands were made famous by Charles Darwin, who visited them in 1835, and was inspired by the diversity of species he found there to develop his theory of evolution. The Galapagos Islands are also known for their stunning natural beauty, with crystal-clear waters, rugged volcanic landscapes, and abundant wildlife.

The Northern Lights (Aurora Borealis), are a natural light display that can be seen in the night sky in the northern hemisphere. They are caused by charged particles colliding with the Earth's atmosphere, which produces a beautiful and colorful display of light. The Northern Lights can be seen in various colors, including green, red, yellow, and blue, and are best viewed from dark and clear locations away from city lights.

91. Oddball

The term "oddball" can be used as a noun to refer to a person who is strange or unusual in some way, or as an adjective to describe something that is unusual or peculiar. One origin theory comes from the idea of a ball that is not perfectly round or symmetrical, and that may be considered unusual or dysfunctional. Another theory is that it may have been derived from the phrase "odd ball," with the word "ball" being used in the sense of "person." In any case, the word "oddball" has been in use in English since at least the 1950s, and it has become a widely used term to describe someone or something that is strange or peculiar.

92. Six of one, half a dozen of other

The idiom "six of one, half a dozen of the other" is used to indicate that two options or alternatives are roughly equal or interchangeable. The earliest known written use of the phrase can be found in the journal of Ralph Clark, a British naval officer, who wrote in 1790 while on a ship in the Pacific Ocean: "Of all the places in the World this is the greatest nest for Rascals it is impossible to trust any one of our men, hardly much more any of the Convicts, in Short there is no difference between Soldier Sailor or Convicts, there Six of the one and half a Dozen of the other." This entry illustrates how the phrase was originally used to describe the equivalence of two different groups of people, but over time, it has become a way to outline the equivalence of any two options.

93. At a crossroads

The term "at a crossroads" describes a situation where a person must make a decision that will have a significant impact on their future. The origin of this phrase comes from physical crossroads, where two or more roads intersect. Historically, crossroads were considered important decision-making points as they offered the opportunity to choose a different direction to travel. A number of ancient tribes utilized crossroads as sites for religious offerings, while during the Christian era, individuals who were executed for crimes and those who perished by their own hand were frequently buried at crossroads. The notion of a symbolic crossroads, a pivotal moment where one must choose the direction to take, has a long history. Erasmus cites a piece from the Elegies of Theognis, a Greek poet from around 600 BC. The quote reads: "I stand at the crossroads" in its English translation.

94. Hail Mary

The phrase "Hail Mary" originated in American football and refers to a last-ditch effort, a desperate or improbable strategy made in the final seconds of a game. Its origins come from the Catholic prayer "Hail Mary" which is a traditional Catholic prayer asking for the intercession of the Virgin Mary, mother of Jesus, when one is in a difficult situation. The idea in American football is that the team member making the play does so while saying a prayer that it will be successful, and is typically when the quarterback throws a long pass into the end-zone in the final seconds before time runs out. The term can be traced back to the 1920s, when it was used by the Four Horsemen of Notre Dame, an outstanding group of players on the college team, to describe a desperate, last-minute forward pass. However, it gained wider use in 1975, when Dallas Cowboys quarterback Roger Staubach made a successful fifty yard pass, later referred to as a Hail Mary pass, during a game. When asked about it later, Staubach said, "I just closed my eyes and said a Hail Mary." This play and the comment brought the term into mainstream use.

95. Hot to trot

The idiom "hot to trot" has its origins in the world of horse racing and horseback riding. The phrase refers to a horse that is ready and eager to run, and was first used in the early 1900s to describe a horse that was yearning to start a race or begin a ride. The expression was later adopted to refer to people who are eager or excited to do something, and is commonly used to portray a person who is enthusiastic or ready to begin a task or activity.

96. Cold-hearted

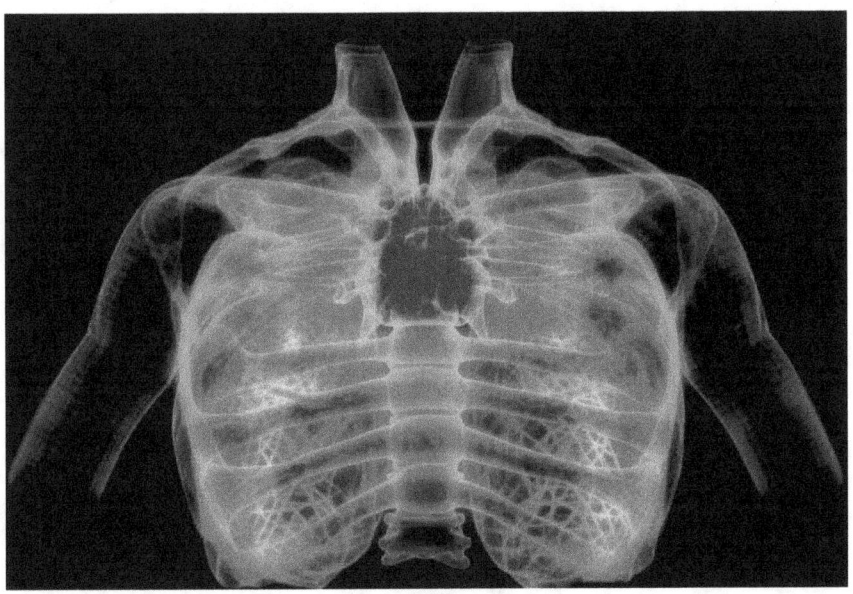

The phrase "cold-hearted" is used to describe a person who is emotionally detached, unsympathetic, or lacking in compassion or empathy. The origin of this idiom comes from the metaphor of comparing a person's emotions to the temperature of the heart. For centuries, people have believed that the heart is the seat of emotions and that a cold-hearted person is one who lacks warmth and compassion in their emotional life. It's important to note that some people might be perceived as cold-hearted due to certain emotional or psychological disorders and not by choice, so this phrase should be used with caution.

97. Clear as mud

The origin of the idiomatic phrase "clear as mud" comes to us from the late 19th century. The idiom is an example of an oxymoron, a figure of speech in which two opposing or contradictory terms are combined. In this case, the word "clear" is used to describe something that is easy to understand, while "mud" is used to represent something that is murky and difficult to see through. The phrase is thought to have originated as a way to express frustration or confusion about something that is supposed to be explained or understood, but is instead difficult to grasp.

98. The devil is in the details

"The devil is in the details" is used to express that small, seemingly insignificant details can cause big problems or difficulties. The phrase originated in the late 19th century, with the earliest citation recorded in the late 1880s. It was first used by Friedrich Wilhelm Nietzsche, a German philosopher and poet, who is quoted as saying "Der Teufel steckt im Detail," which translates to "The devil is in the details." Nietzsche's use of the expression may have been a play on the original phrase "God is in the details," which means that a higher power has a hand in the success and truthfulness of a completed work. Nowadays, when we say "the devil is in the details," it has a similar connotation to "read the fine print" or "pay attention" in that it is a warning to be on the lookout for the small, often forgotten things.

99. Take to the cleaners

The idiom "to take to the cleaners" means to cheat or defraud someone out of a large amount of money or resources. It is frequently used in the context of gambling or legal disputes, where one person threatens to beat the other in a gamble or to sue them in court. The phrase is thought to have evolved from an older idiom, "to clean someone out," which means to strip someone of their money. It is believed to have come into use in the 1920s, around the time when dry cleaning establishments began to crop up. The metaphor of cleaning or laundering money is often used to refer to situations where someone is taken advantage of or duped in a way that leaves them financially or materially worse off. The earliest written use of this expression appears in *The New Dictionary of American Slang* by Harold Wentworth and Stuart Berg Flexner, which was published in 1960.

100. If worse comes to worst

When someone says "if worse comes to worst," it means that they are preparing for the least desirable outcome, almost with resignation that it will come true. This idiom dates back to 1596, in a pamphlet written by Thomas Dash in which he compared dying by drowning versus dying by burning. He wrote, "If the worst comes to the worst, a good swimmer may do much." The phrase has since been used by the likes of Charles Dickens and Charlotte Brontë. Initially, the idiom presented the idea of a worst-case hypothetical scenario that becomes a reality. In 1719, Daniel Defoe wrote *Robinson Crusoe* and used a slightly altered version of the expression when the titular character said, "If the worse came to the worst, I could but die." The term gained a more negative connotation, as it hints that the situation is already negative and has the possibility of becoming more so.

Did You Know?

There are more stars in the observable universe than there are grains of sand on all the beaches on Earth. The observable universe is estimated to contain around two trillion galaxies, each of which contains billions of stars. The exact number of stars in the universe is not known, but it is estimated to be in the hundreds of billions of billions, making it impossible to count the number of stars in the observable universe. The estimated number of grains of sand on all the beaches on Earth, on the other hand, is estimated to be around 7.5×10^{18}.

One light-year is the distance that light travels in one year. Light travels at a speed of 299,792,458 meters per second (in a vacuum), making it the fastest thing in the universe. A light-year is the distance that light travels in one year, which is approximately 5.88 trillion miles (9.46 trillion kilometers).

The Sun is one of over a hundred billion stars in the Milky Way galaxy. The Milky Way is a barred spiral galaxy that is part of the Local Group of galaxies, which also includes the Andromeda Galaxy, the Triangulum Galaxy, and about fifty-four other smaller galaxies. The Sun is located in one of the spiral arms of the Milky Way and it is estimated that there are at least 100 billion stars in our galaxy alone, with possibly even more undiscovered.

A black hole is formed when a massive star collapses under the force of its own gravity. The gravitational pull of a black hole is so strong that it does not allow anything, not even light, to escape once it has crossed the event horizon. The event horizon is the point of no return, beyond which anything that enters is pulled into the black hole, never to escape again. Black holes are some of the most mysterious and fascinating objects in the universe, and scientists are still learning about their properties and behaviors.

101. Graveyard shift

The phrase "graveyard shift" refers to a work schedule that takes place during the overnight hours, typically from midnight to 8 a.m. The idea of a shift in the middle of the night being like a graveyard is likely a metaphor, as night is when everyone else (working a normal shift) is sleeping, the streets are deserted, and the world is as quiet as a graveyard. The expression "graveyard shift" originated in the US in the late 1800s, as mine and factory owners discovered they could increase production by operating twenty-four hours a day. The term conveys a less-than-favorable schedule and hints at the worker missing out on a typical social life.

Bonus!

Thanks for supporting me and purchasing this book! I'd like to send you some freebies. They include:

- The digital version of *500 World War I & II Facts*

- The digital version of *101 Idioms and Phrases*

- The audiobook for my best seller *1144 Random Facts*

Scan the QR code below, enter your email and I'll send you all the files. Happy reading!

Check out my other books!

www.ingramcontent.com/pod-product-compliance
Lightning Source LLC
Chambersburg PA
CBHW070048230426
43661CB00005B/807